AYO'S **AWESOME** ADVENTURES IN

BEIJING

CAPITAL OF CHINA

WORLD BOOK

www.worldbook.com

World Book, Inc.
180 North LaSalle Street
Suite 900
Chicago, Illinois 60601
USA

For information about other World Book publications, visit our website at www.worldbook.com or call 1-800-WORLDBK (967-5325).

For information about sales to schools and libraries, call 1-800-975-3250 (United States), or 1-800-837-5365 (Canada).

Library of Congress Cataloging-in-Publication Data for this volume has been applied for.

Ayo's Awesome Adventures
ISBN: 978-0-7166-3636-6 (set, hc.)

Ayo's Awesome Adventures in Beijing:
Capital of China
ISBN: 978-0-7166-3637-3 (hc.)

Also available as:
ISBN: 978-0-7166-3648-9 (e-book)

1st printing July 2018

Staff

Writer: Kim O'Connor

Executive Committee

President
Jim O'Rourke

Vice President and
Editor in Chief
Paul A. Kobasa

Vice President, Finance
Donald D. Keller

Vice President, Marketing
Jean Lin

Vice President, International Sales
Maksim Rutenberg

Vice President, Technology
Jason Dole

Director, Human Resources
Bev Ecker

Editorial

Director, New Print
Tom Evans

Managing Editor, New Print
Jeff De La Rosa

Series Editor
Nathalie Strassheim

Librarian
S. Thomas Richardson

Manager, Contracts & Compliance
(Rights & Permissions)
Loranne K. Shields

Manager, Indexing Services
David Pofelski

Digital

Director, Digital Product
Development
Erika Meller

Manager, Digital Products
Jonathan Wills

Graphics and Design

Senior Art Director
Tom Evans

Senior Visual Communications
Designer
Melanie Bender

Senior Web Designer/Digital
Media Developer
Matthew Carrington

Media Researcher
Rosalia Bledsoe

Senior Cartographer
John M. Rejba

**Manufacturing/
Production**

Manufacturing Manager
Anne Fritzinger

Proofreaders
Mary Kieffer
Georgina Milsted

Contents

Introduction

Are you ready for an adventure? My name is Ayo. I'm an aardvark, an African mammal that eats ants and termites. I'm also a tour guide

traveling the world. I hope you will come with me. We are going to explore cities around the globe.

Today we will visit the city of Beijing. Maybe you have never heard that name before. Let's say it together. It sounds like *bay jihng*.

Beijing is the capital of China. China is a country on the continent of Asia. Africa is my home continent. Aren't you curious about my name? *Ayo* comes from an African word meaning *joy*.

On our visit, we'll read and hear words that may be new to you. Some of these words will be in a language called Mandarin. Most people in Beijing speak Mandarin.

If I can explain what a word means easily, I'll do it right where you are reading. If I use the word many times, or if the explanation is complicated, I will put the word in boldface (type that **looks like this).** Boldface words are defined in a glossary in the back of the book.

I'll also try to sound out any words you may not have heard before. We already tried one together, remember? Beijing *(bay jihng).*

I hope someday you will travel with your family to Beijing. You can ask to see the places we visit in this book! Then you can be the tour guide for your parents and brothers and sisters.

A S I A

BEIJING •

China

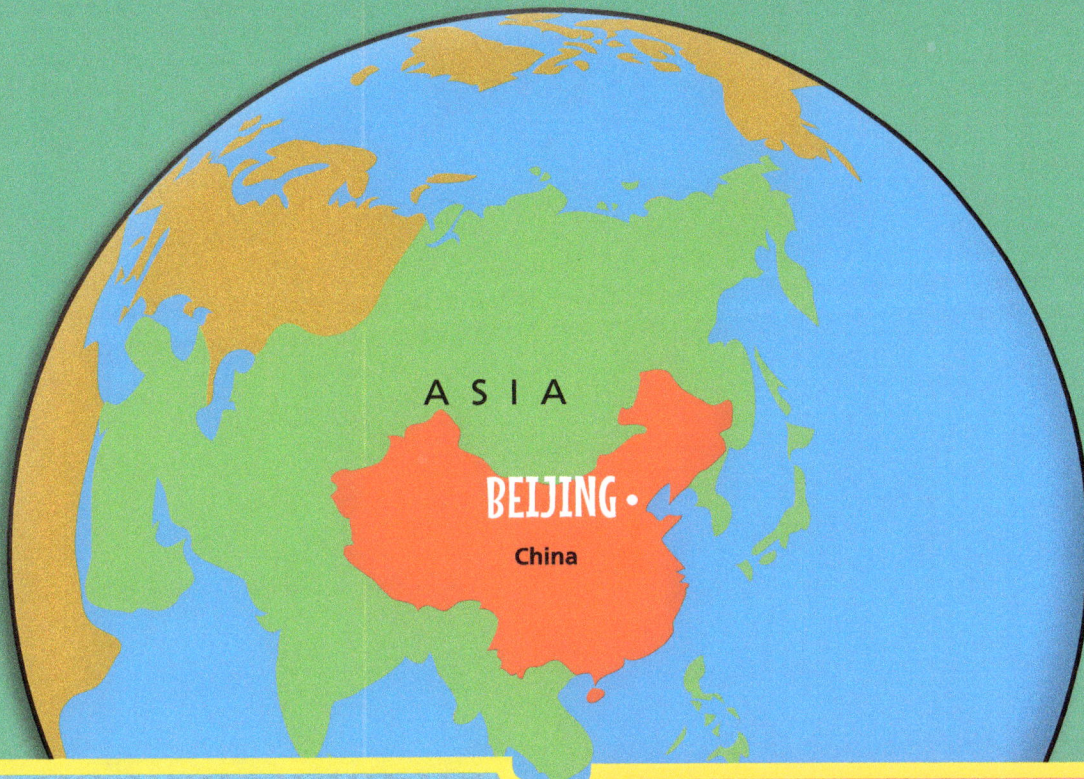

Beijing information

- Population: 11,509,595

- Founded: Around 2000 B.C.

- Very old and very new: Beijing is one of the world's oldest cities—about 4,000 years old! Many of the buildings popular with tourists are hundreds of years old. But Beijing is also a modern city. It has modern skyscrapers, bright lights, and busy industry.

China information

- Climate: Northeastern China (where Beijing is located) has cold, dry winters and hot, humid summers.

- Money: Yuan (also called renminbi). One hundred fen equal one yuan.

- Flag: The big star stands for the leadership of the Communist Party. The four small stars stand for groups of workers.

flag of China

The Great Wall

Let's begin just north of Beijing. I want to show you one of the most amazing things ever built—the Great Wall. This part of the wall is on Mount Badaling. We can get there by bus, train, or car from the city center.

For much of its history, China was ruled by **emperors.** They had the wall built to protect the country from invaders. It was built in parts over hundreds of years. This part was finished in 1505. It has been kept up to show us what the wall was like when it was built. Other parts of the wall are also still standing, but some have crumbled. There are spots along the path of the wall where hills, rivers, or other natural barriers take the place of the wall.

The wall stands 35 feet (11 meters) tall here. Enemies from outside would have had a hard time getting over it. We can get to the top by climbing stairs or riding the cable car. It is like a little car that hangs from a long wire called a cable.

We can't walk along the entire wall. It stretches for nearly 5,500 miles (8,850 kilometers)! But we can visit the Great Wall Museum. There, we can learn how the Great Wall was built. Then, we can head back toward the city center.

Tiananmen Square

We're now at the center of Beijing, in Tiananmen (pronounced *tee AH nuhn mehn*) Square. This is the biggest public square in the whole world. I've heard that a million people can fit here.

Tiananmen Square is mostly wide open space. There is no place to sit and rest. There are no trees for shade. There are a lot of people walking around, though. One thing people like to do here is fly kites!

The square may seem pretty empty now. But in the city's history, crowds have gathered here for important events. **Emperors** and **empresses** once held ceremonies here. This has also been the site of huge political

Tiananmen Gate

gatherings and other events.

On the west side of the square is the Great Hall of the People. The Chinese government meets in this huge building. That giant stone pillar is called the Monument to the People's Heroes. To the east of the square is the National Museum of China.

Let's head north to the Tiananmen Gate, also known as the Gate of Heavenly Peace. A picture of Mao Zedong (pronounced *mow zeh dawng)* hangs in front. Mao (1893-1976) was the founder of China's modern, **communist** government. If we come to the gate at sunrise, we can watch a ceremony to raise the country's flag.

The Forbidden City

On the other side of the gate, we'll find a special place. It's called the Forbidden City. *Forbidden* means *off limits*. Hundreds of years ago, guards would have stopped us from entering. Now anyone can visit.

The Forbidden City was the home of the **emperor.** The common people were not allowed inside. China was ruled by emperors for thousands of years. The last emperor was a six-year-old boy. This child stopped being emperor in 1912 because of a revolution. The country is now ruled by a **communist** government.

What will we see in the Forbidden City?

- Giant halls
- Big courtyards
- Pretty gardens
- Special temples
- Marble sundials
- Opera houses
- Fancy carvings
- Colorful paintings
- Animal sculptures

Today, the Forbidden City is a huge museum called the Palace Museum. It is surrounded by walls and a *moat*—a ditch filled with water. The main entrance is the gigantic Meridian Gate. It stands 12 stories over us! When emperors lived here, the Meridian Gate was for them only. Bells and gongs would ring when they came through it. Other people who were allowed into the Forbidden City had to enter through smaller gates. We are allowed to use the Meridian Gate now. Let's go through it.

Inside the gate, there is a large courtyard. The first thing to do is cross over the Golden Stream. There are five marble bridges. Which one do you want to take? This part of the Forbidden City is called the Outer Court. On the other side, the three most important buildings are right in a row. They are named the Hall of Supreme Harmony, the Hall of Middle Harmony, and the Hall of Preserving Harmony. Many ceremonies and rituals took place in these halls long ago.

Let's visit the **emperor's** throne room. It's in the Hall of Supreme Harmony. All the posts holding up the roof look like a forest, don't they? Each is made from a single enormous tree trunk. There seem to be pictures of a certain animal everywhere. No, those aren't aardvarks—they're dragons! Dragons are carved into wood, sculpted from stone, and painted on floors and furniture.

Many of these buildings are more than 600 years old. The entire Forbidden City was built in just 14 years! There are more than 800 buildings altogether, so that was quick work. Today, workers are *restoring* many of the buildings. That means they are making the buildings look like they did when they were first built.

Dragons in China are thought of as being friendly and bringing good luck. We don't have to be scared.

throne room

建極綏猷

天心佑夫一德永言配□□

帝命武于九圍茲惟艱哉戰兢

15

Past the Outer Court is the Inner Court. The **emperor's** family lived in these buildings. Everywhere we turn there's another display of interesting things, such as clocks or huge carvings of *jade*. Jade is a hard, brightly colored stone. It is prized in China and elsewhere. The displays are in buildings with cool names. We can visit the House of Joyful *Longevity* (long life, pronounced *lon JEHV uh tee*) or the Pavilion of Cheerful Melodies, to name just two!

You probably noticed that the rooftops are a golden yellow. Hundreds of years ago, Chinese law said that only the emperor could use the color yellow. **Beijingers** knew the tall buildings with yellow roofs belonged to the emperor.

Most of the buildings here are made of wood, and fire was a danger. Even the big halls burned several times. Big metal pots, called *urns,* held water to put out any fires. Some of the urns are still here.

Animal helpers

- All around the Forbidden City, there are lots of animal helpers. (They are statues, not real animals like me.)

- Lions guard important buildings.

- Bronze turtles hold fragrant **incense.**

- Water spouts look like dragon heads.

lion guarding
a building

Beihai Park

Let's leave the Forbidden City through the North Gate. This is the gate that was used by servants. It's just a short walk to Beihai *(bay HEYE)* Park. Before the Forbidden City was built, **emperors** lived in a palace here. The palace is long gone, but there are other things to see.

Do you see the man painting on the ground with a giant brush? He is practicing *calligraphy (kuh LIHG ruh fee),* the art of fancy writing. Chinese language can be written with characters, rather than letters. Some characters look like little pictures. See how the characters begin to fade after he draws them? His brush holds water, rather than ink. As the water evaporates, the characters fade.

The next thing I want to show you is across the lake. Instead of walking along the shore, let's take a paddleboat. Here's one that is shaped like a big yellow duck. A grownup can help us get to the northwest shore.

We don't have to walk far to see the Nine Dragon Screen. Do you see the long wall with the blue background? Old legends say that walls like this made mean ghosts turn away. Dragons and ghosts are in many old Chinese stories.

Hutongs

From Beihai Park, we can take a bus to a *hutong* (pronounced *HOO tawng).* Hutongs are narrow streets between buildings. Most hutongs are too narrow for cars or buses, so we'll go the rest of the way on foot. It feels a little bit like a maze, doesn't it? Watch out for people riding bikes and motorcycles. Sometimes they zoom past at high speed.

There once were many more hutongs in Beijing. Then the city was chosen to host the 2008 Summer Olympics. People changed the city to prepare for all the visitors from other countries. Many hutongs were removed to make room for new buildings.

There are lots of food smells in the air. I see little markets where people buy vegetables and other items. There are also small stalls that sell snacks. Most of the foods are on small wooden sticks called *skewers.* How about a candy-coated apple? Or perhaps a deep-fried scorpion? Don't worry about the stinger. It's cooked all the way through. Some people think a scorpion tastes like fried chicken skin.

Fried street snacks

Hutongs are known as places to find unusual snacks. Are you brave enough to try one?

- Centipedes
- Giant insects
- Sea horses
- Snakes
- Starfish
- Spiders

Drum and Bell towers

The two buildings just ahead are the Drum and Bell towers. How do we know which is which? Easy! The gray building is the Bell Tower, and the red building is the Drum Tower.

Hundreds of years ago, before all these skyscrapers, the Drum and Bell towers were some of the tallest buildings around. The sounds of bells and drums helped people to keep the time. Bells rang in the morning, and the drums were played at nighttime.

Let's go in the Bell Tower first. We can take steep steps to the second floor. Did I tell you the bell at the top weighs more than a herd of elephants? It's also 600 years old! The thing I like most here is the view. We can see the Drum Tower through a big window.

Do you hear that? I think people are playing the drums in the other tower. We can go watch, if you want to huff and puff up another set of stairs. Quickly! The drums are only played a handful of times a day for a few minutes. There are 25 of them. When the show is over, we can walk to the subway station. There, we'll catch a train to our next stop.

Temple of Heaven

When you think of a temple, you may imagine a big building. The Temple of Heaven is really a park with many buildings.

The park's shape has special meaning. It is square in the south and rounded in the north. People in ancient China thought of Earth as square and the Heavens as round. So the park's shape is a symbol of the connection, or link, between Earth and the Heavens.

Emperors once came here to say special prayers. They paraded through the south gate. Shall we have our own parade?

Chinese emperors were called the "sons of heaven." Everyone thought they could talk to the gods. They could ask for big favors, such as good weather for growing crops. In fact, see this round building with the blue roof? It is called the Hall of Prayer for Good Harvests.

When you look inside, see if you can spot the pillars. There are 28 in all. They are made from fir trees from Oregon, a U.S. state. The hall burned down in 1889. People rebuilt it soon after, using trees from Oregon. My favorite part is the carved dragon, right in the middle of the ceiling.

Chopstick manners

People in China use chopsticks in place of forks, knives, and spoons. They are used like pincers to pick up the food. If you haven't used them before, you might drop a few things at first. Don't worry—you just need a little more practice.

t'ai chi

Beijingers and tourists come to the Temple of Heaven to enjoy the sunshine. I see a group of people making slow, smooth movements with their bodies. I think they're practicing *t'ai chi* (ty jee). T'ai chi is a form of ancient Chinese exercise.

Look up! The Temple of Heaven is a great place to fly kites. The first kites were probably invented in China more than 2,000 years ago. They weren't big pink jellyfish or other fun shapes like we have today. They were mostly square. They were made from bamboo and a kind of cloth called silk. I like jellyfish kites better.

Are you hungry? After we leave, we can stop for *dim sum.* It's a meal made up of many small dishes. In restaurants, dim sum is served from carts wheeled around the dining room. We can just point at whatever we want. Would you like to try dumplings? They are little pouches of dough filled with meats and vegetables.

Lama Temple

It's a short train ride from the Temple of Heaven to the Lama Temple. The Lama Temple is different from the Temple of Heaven. It is a place of worship and a lamasery, or *monastery*. A monastery is where monks live while they study and practice religion. People here practice a kind of religion called **Buddhism.** The monks who live here are called *lamas*.

There are five main halls arranged from south to north. Our walk through them is a symbol of the journey from Earth to heaven. All around are statues of the religion's founder, the Buddha (pronounced *BOO duh)*. There are so many that I've already lost count! The biggest one is in the final hall. It towers over us! But there is even more of it that we can't see. Some of it sticks into the ground. The whole thing is 60 feet (18 meters) tall—so big that the hall was built around it.

What's all that smoke? It comes from **incense** burning at the temple's altars. Keep an eye out for lamas, with their bright robes and shaved heads. Most people here are worshipers or tourists, though.

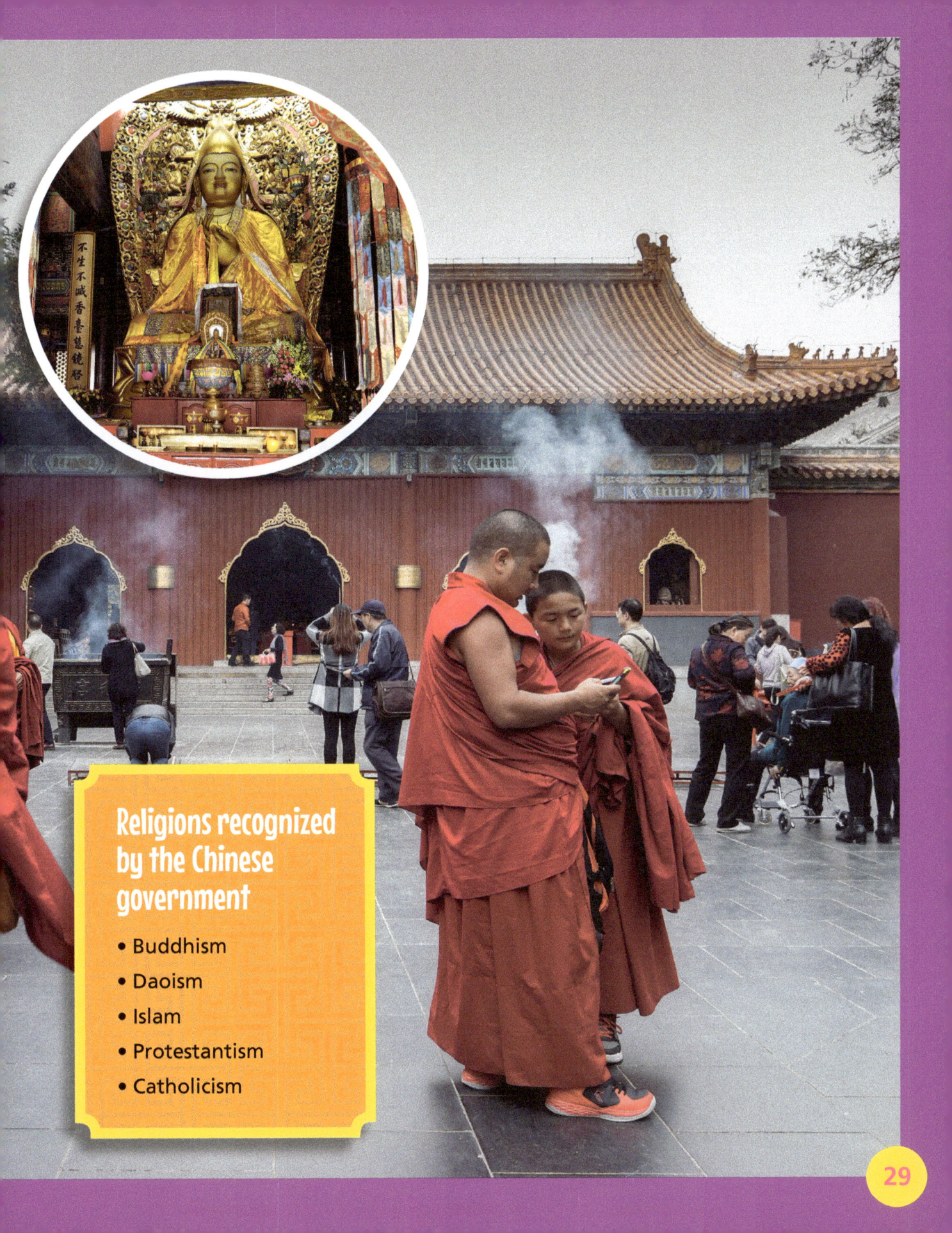

Religions recognized by the Chinese government

- Buddhism
- Daoism
- Islam
- Protestantism
- Catholicism

The Beijing Zoo

There are thousands of animals at the Beijing Zoo. But we're here to see one very special kind of animal. It's black and white and big and furry. Can you guess what it is? That's right! We're going to see the giant pandas. We don't need to read signs to find the panda house. We can just follow the crowd. Giant pandas are very popular. If the zoo were a show, the pandas would be its stars.

Wild giant pandas live only in the mountains of central China. Giant pandas love to eat…and eat…and eat. They eat for up to 12 hours a day! Giant pandas eat only bamboo, so I guess they won't want this sack of ants I packed for our snack. Bamboo is a kind of giant grass with big leaves and woody stems. Giant pandas have to eat about 85 pounds (40 kilograms) of it a day.

There aren't many giant pandas left in the wild, and there aren't many in zoos, either. We are lucky to see them here.

red panda

Who else lives here?

- Red pandas from the bamboo forests
- Tigers from Siberia
- Sea turtles from the coast of China
- Yaks from Tibet

Summer Palace

Our next stop is on the edge of the city, so let's take a taxi. I'll ask the driver to take us to the Summer Palace. **Emperors** and their families used to come to the Summer Palace for vacation. Most of the palace grounds are taken up by Kunming Lake. We can walk around the lake or take an electric boat out on the water.

Most of the buildings are on the northern shore. Let's walk down the Long Corridor. It's like a big outdoor hallway. The sides are open so we can see the water. The ceiling over our heads is covered with beautiful paintings. I don't see any aardvarks in them, though. Many scenes are from Chinese history or mythology, and there are no aardvarks in China. We could spend all day here crossing bridges, visiting temples, and exploring palace halls. The main buildings rise up the side of Longevity Hill, looking over Kunming Lake.

The Old Summer Palace is just a few blocks away. French and British soldiers destroyed it in 1860. Now it looks like an ancient ruin. Be careful! We don't want to trip on the broken stone statues and columns.

Let's try to find our way through the Yellow Flower Maze at the Old Summer Palace. This giant maze has concrete walls. Our job is to find the building, called a pavilion, in the middle. The maze was rebuilt after being destroyed in 1860.

Long Corridor

Tea Street

Let's return to the heart of the city, to a street called Maliandao *(MA lee AHN dow).* It's also known as Tea Street, which is easier to say. This is a huge market where people come to buy tea. There are more than 1,000 shops and teahouses lining the street. That's a lot of tea!

Did you know that tea was invented in China? Thousands of years ago, it was even used as money. Tea is still a popular Chinese drink. That's why there are so many shops here.

Take a deep breath. There are good smells everywhere. Tea has a soft, pleasant scent. There are different kinds on the shelves of each stall. Some of the tea is pressed into round discs. They look like little Frisbees wrapped in paper. The woman at the next stall is trying to get our attention! Maybe she wants to give us a free, hot sample!

Did you know there are different colors of tea? Here they have green tea, and they have red tea (the kind called black tea in many English-speaking countries). There is tea made of flower petals! Let's try green tea first.

Acrobats, puppets, and martial arts

Now that we've had a tea break, let's go out on the town! I think we should see a show, but it might be hard to choose. We could watch the acrobats. Acrobats have been jumping, bending, balancing, and twisting in China for thousands of years. A fun place to see a show is the Tianquiao *(tee AHN kee OW)* Acrobatics Theater. It's about 100 years old. It is very close to the Temple of Heaven's west gate. We should have a good view, because the theater is small.

How about a puppet show? Shadow puppets were invented in China. These puppets are used to cast shadows on a screen. A master will work the puppets, while a singer sings the story. We'll hear music made by cymbals, drum blocks, and an *erhu* (pronounced *AIR oo)*, a stringed instrument. Chinese people have enjoyed puppet shows for more than 2,000 years.

I have another idea! We could see a demonstration of *martial* (fighting) arts, sometimes called *kung fu*. In China, such arts are called *wu shu*. Wu shu is more than fighting. It's an art—like dancing, but with cooler kicks.

I know what we should do! Let's go to the opera.

acrobatics show

Martial arts weapons

- Wooden staffs
- Pointy spears
- Long swords
- Short knives

Opera

Opera is a kind of musical play. The performers in an opera sing most of their lines, rather than speaking them. Many cities have one opera house. In Beijing, there are hundreds. Chinese opera may sound strange to your ears. You may have a hard time telling different songs apart. But wait until you hear more of it. Your ears will get used to the new sounds.

Some kinds of opera are performed by men alone and some by women. Let's find a performance with a mix of people. Chinese opera singers must have many different skills. They must sing, often dance, and sometimes even do martial arts! The acting is complicated. The singing alone can take 10 years to learn!

One last thing: the costumes are very fancy. The costumers make them from shiny, colorful fabrics. They sew patterns and shapes on them with colorful thread. (This kind of sewing is called *embroidery*.) Once the show is over, we can talk about which ones we liked best.

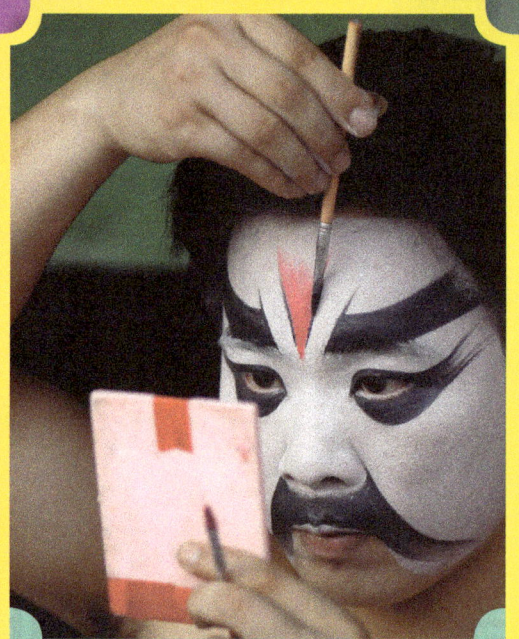

Face paint

The performers wear face paint in bright colors. The colors tell us about the character. Red is used for heroes. Bad guys wear white face paint. (White is an unlucky color in China.) Green is used for characters who fight.

Dinner

I'm getting hungry. Should we get dinner? Let's try a small restaurant. We can choose where to sit. The server gave us only one menu. In China, one person orders for the whole table. Dishes are big, so everyone can share. All the food is served hot and fresh. The server will bring each dish to our table as soon as it's ready.

China is a big country with many styles of cooking. The most famous dish in Beijing is called Peking duck. (*Peking* is an old name for Beijing.) We roll up the duck meat in a thin pancake. It looks like a taco, but the taste is more sweet than spicy.

mayi shang shu

I will also order mayi shang shu (*may yee SHANG shu*). In English, that means *ants climbing a tree*. It doesn't have real ants like I eat at home, but it's close enough. Those little dark things on the noodles are pieces of tasty pork, not ants. Let's get our chopsticks ready. Do you remember how to use them?

The server will bring us steaming cups of tea. Most **Beijingers** drink hot tea with their meal, instead of water.

Panjiayuan Market

Are you full after our feast? Let's take one last walk. We can stop at the Panjiayuan *(PAN zhuh yoo AHN)* Market, one of the most famous places to shop in Beijing. It's almost all outside. Everything for sale is spread out on rugs or stacked on shelves. Each seller has a small area.

When you shop in a Chinese market, you have to work hard to get a good deal. The customer is expected to *bargain,* or try to get a better price. Let's say I want to buy some

termites. "These termites don't look juicy enough," I might say and turn to leave. The seller may offer a cheaper price to lure me back.

There are thousands of sellers here on busy days. I see items of all shapes and sizes. There are tiny carvings and huge statues. There are delicate vases. Rugs and furniture come in all different colors. Let's pick a souvenir for you to take home. A teapot might fit in your suitcase.

Hutongs

Summer
Palace

Forbidden
City

The Great Wall

Beijing Zoo

Thanks for
exploring Beijing
with me. I hope to
see you soon!

Ayo

Glossary

Beijinger *(bay ZHING er)* A person who lives in the city of Beijing

Buddhism *(BOO dihz uhm)* A religion started in India by a man named Siddhartha Gautama. His followers called him the Buddha, which means Enlightened One. An enlightened person is someone who is wise, fair, and thoughtful.

communism *(KAHM yoo nihs uhm)* A form of government in which the government controls land, factories, and other ways to make money

emperor *(EHM per ohr)* The ruler of a large area, sometimes a group of nations or states

empress *(EHM prihs)* The wife of an emperor or a female emperor

incense *(IHN sehns)* A mixture of spices and other substances that smells sweet and gives off smoke when burned

Acknowledgments

Cover © TonyV3112/Shutterstock
Ayo artwork by Matthew Carrington

4-23   © Shutterstock
24-25 © fotoVoyager/iStockphoto; © ONEShutterStock/Shutterstock
26-27 © Bruno Barbier, age footstock; ©Shutterstock; © Religious Images/UIG/Getty Images
28-39 © Shutterstock
40-41 © Gareth Morgans, StockFood/age footstock; © Andrew Furlong Photography/iStockphoto
42-43 © Shutterstock

Index

For further reading

Books

Manzione, Lisa. *Let's Visit Beijing: Adventures of Bella & Harry.* Bella & Harry: Palm Beach County, 2015.

Paris, Harper. *The Mystery in the Forbidden City (Greetings from Somewhere).* Little Simon: New York, 2014.

Platt, Richard. *Through Time: Beijing.* Kingfisher: New York, 2008.

Websites

"China." National Geographic Kids.
http://kids.nationalgeographic.com/explore/countries/china/#china-dragon.jpg

"The Story of China: Map."
http://www.pbs.org/story-china/map/#/intro

"Time Out: Beijing for Families."
http://www.timeoutbeijing.com/family.html